# Orange & Blue

Paul Bowden

BookLeaf Publishing

Presentation by *BookLeaf Publishing*

Web: www.bookleafpub.com

E-mail: info@bookleafpub.com


ISBN: 9789395969499

First edition 2022

# La Projector

tragic relationships
so many
project on
the beloved other
traumatic endless failures

therapy is about
trust
strategic relationship alternatives
on our
overwhelmed
or
abandoned trauma

# Koriander

silent

war

voice
clear and
cold

back and forth
training
an
army
camp there

rifle structures

they dumbstruck fire ground their wooden
spaces

he saddles a metal form
from these there be a dug end

# Third La

arrows, arrows
protect them, spare us
discover strengths
and vulnerabilities
gifts offered
will cure loneliness
learning that
we
share ourselves
to receive their gifts

# For Her

frozen earth
fire
choking
water spills
desperate to claim the days
you compose six-eight-time music
for her to kiss
the song
at dusk
kindling inner
mangled
fire

# Dish It Out in the Cold

men and women
speaking
tones

cuss
fire
and aim

seek out
post
metal in a smile
stifle it

he studied war
weapons drawn
scruff and grime
of her own beauty:

dark blue eyes

# Special Love

begin
the relationship
over again, love

work
reflect
own
and sort
the worn fantasy

"love"
take responsibility
for meeting more
of his or her
needs

profess love
become the presence of
healing

work frequently:
mutual activity

wise being sit

# Camera Obscura

I became
the sound of
vivid color
passing in the opposite
window
placing my eye
on the other side
and the garden image
turned upside down

I walk back
and experiment
this vivid illusion
I called inside
walking the visual effects

both of us
a rare event
like a camera obscura
soothing the soul

# Beyond, in Sight

beyond the
wooden
beyond moss-covered wonders
the lady's impressive garden
design
provided many windows

hard to believe it
original moon viewing hills
obstructed its residents
destroy the elegant
windows
had a relaxing effect on the weary

of the horizon
the owner's garden ran on
beyond
windows to speak
of the residence
features of the land

eyes fell over
oblique sunlight
like an avalanche

# Avant-Garde

in the light dream
he found
refuge in music
and much passion

I think
my notebooks
attracted the time

I am looking at
avant-garde music
suddenly animated
come to life

decades of analytic practice
such intrapsychic images
mythic movements hum

# The Dream

the dream
the passage
of charged effort

the dreamer naturally
expresses
feels
psychic
his relationship to the inner world
he attracted his life
so clear

encourage discussion
find a transformative element
creative expression
animated soul springs to life
value of music embodies
a life he loves

# Danger in Detachment

several months later, I
was brought
to the point of novel death
and sold in bookstores

not in touch with me again
stricken
with anger and grief
resentment arrived on top
of that,
it made things all the more complicated

resentment?

an estranged alienating feeling
as if abducted by resentment
but a piece of writing,
no matter how you interpret it,
the act of writing is
a way to cleanse and
to purify

# Invisible Thoughts

night mutters the music
for him
music of invisible thoughts
lonesome, but
musical gifts
made him feel less
alone

he hummed about
the past
again, he seems to know
his smile feels shy
he returns his smile quickly then

at the start,
one eagle
decorated with time
sewn into being
didn't jangle

do you know
he practices as best he can

# Perhaps

perhaps
the conversation is
dead
silent dreaming hours
gather and test
the fog of hunger
finds real pants
a bit energized
took soap
starting fires
in the woods

# Each Morning, Fly to the Garden

each morning
fly

waterfall
hung midair

read book
near water

utter the word "friend"
flew away

awkwardly hanging out
one day
near the end of August

a female rested
like a bracelet
shape of heart

them
they flew without breaking formation
to the garden

observe the heart
dance away in the sky above

# Attack of the Ping-Pong Ball

15

The year 3003 arrived
it was
night?

it had become my greatest life
no matter how cold the climb

a ping-pong ball would attack
never tire
it follow
wherever he wanted to go
mounting the stairs
into a great hollow shell of darkness

study the grand old moonlight
bathe in it and
let it embrace your soul

# Possibility is Alive?

the forest calls
possibility is alive?
a window to see
begin on ventures
find footing
step out of path
determined
call kindly
stiffen heel
circling hours
the photo from pocket
remember her among them?
I'm sorry, I don't know
a girl looks discomfited

# Fearful Flickerings

sewn wonderful
pants
for traveling
scents sounds
screech and whistle
fearful flickerings
to share this project
along the road
through zooming out

cello set to whole notes
the violin voice
creeks and rivers
whisper of tides

# Atlas of Winter's Light

friends meandered
in and out of the music
striking deep-angled
lyrical movement
hums
bouncy notes
spirit most eager
one quiet collision
atlas of winter's light
may keep
the pages colored
in pale brown
in green
sea blue immensely
do you see?

# Graze in the Fields

so
questions of spirituality
are living in us
the false self is
afraid to go to hell
people feel guilty
any bondage to fear
is violence to the soul
our selves are too small
God resonates true meaning
graze in the fields
as our fellow creatures do

www.ingramcontent.com/pod-product-compliance
Lightning Source LLC
Chambersburg PA
CBHW061331140726
47998CB00007B/2646